STEPHEN ALBERT

SUN'S HEAT
from *Distant Hills*

(piano reduction)

ED-3820

First printing: February 1993

G. SCHIRMER, Inc.

DISTRIBUTED BY

7777 W. BLUEMOUND RD. P.O. BOX 13819 MILWAUKEE, WI 53213

"Sun's Heat"

Those girls, those girls, etc., those lovely seaside girls.
Sharp as needles they are.
Eyes all over them.
Longing to get the fright of their lives,
Those girls, those lovely seaside girls.
Allow me to introduce my.
Have their own secrets.
Those girls, those girls, those lovely seaside girls.
Chaps that would go to the dogs if some woman didn't take them in hand.

Wait.

Hm Hm Yes-that's her perfume.
What is it? Heliotrope?
Know her smell in a thousand.
Bath water, too.
Reminds me of strawberries, and cream.
Hyacinth perfume made of oil or ether or something.
Muscrat. That's her perfume.

Dogs at each other behind.
How do you sniff?
Hm, Hm. Animals go by that
Yes now,
Dogs at each other behind,
Good evening. Evening.
Yes now, look at it that way we're the same.

Just close my eyes a moment won't sleep though.
Half dream. She kissed me.
Half dream. My youth.

It's the blood of the south.
Moorish.
Also the form. The figure.
Just close my eyes, half dream,
She kissed me, kissed me, kissed me.
Sun's heat it is seems to a secret touch telling me memory.

Below us bay sleeping sky,
No sound.
The sky.
The bay purple fields of under sea . . . buried cities.
Pillowed on my coat she had her hair
Earwigs in the heather scrub,
my hand under her nape, you'll toss me all.
O wonder! Softly she gave me in my mouth seed-cake warm and chewed
Joy: I ate it: Joy.
Young life her lips that gave me pouting.
Flowers her eyes were, take me, willing eyes.
All yielding she tossed my hair,
Kissed, she kissed me.
Willing eyes all yielding.
Me. And me now.

Dew falling. The year returns.
Ye crags and peaks I'm with you once again.
The distant hills seem.
Where we.
The rhododendrons
All that old hill has seen
All changed forgotten.
And the distant hills seem coming nigh.
A star I see
Were those night clouds there all the time?
No. Wait.
Trees are they?
Mirage.

—JAMES JOYCE (Excerpts from *Ulysses*)

Used by arrangement with The Society of Authors as the literary representative of the Estate of James Joyce

Sun's Heat (chamber version) was commissioned by the Chamber Music Society of Lincoln Center and given its first performance on April 27, 1990 with David Gordon, tenor, and Christopher Kendall, conductor. On February 8, 1991, the New York Chamber Symphony premiered the full orchestra version with Mark Bleeke, tenor, and Gerard Schwarz, conductor.

This work may be performed as the first movement of a larger work entitled *Distant Hills*. The second movement of this larger work is titled *Flower of the Mountain* and employs a soprano soloist with either a chamber or orchestral accompaniment. The text of both works is taken from Joyce's *Ulysses*.

INSTRUMENTATION
Chamber Version

Flute (doubling Alto Flute)
Oboe
Clarinet in B♭ (doubling Clarinet in A)
Bassoon

Horn in F

Piano

Violin I
Violin II
Viola
Cello
Bass

Orchestra Version

2 Flutes
2 Oboes
2 Clarinets in B♭
2 Bassoons

2 Horns in F
2 Trumpets in B♭

Timpani
Percussion (1 player): Glockenspiel, Vibraphone, Chimes, Bass Drum

Piano
Harp

Strings

duration: ca. 15 minutes

The orchestral score of *Flower of the Mountain* is available for purchase, no. 50488736

Orchestra material for both the chamber and orchestra version is available on rental from the publisher.

for my friend David Gordon

SUN'S HEAT

from *Distant Hills*

James Joyce

Stephen Albert
(1989)

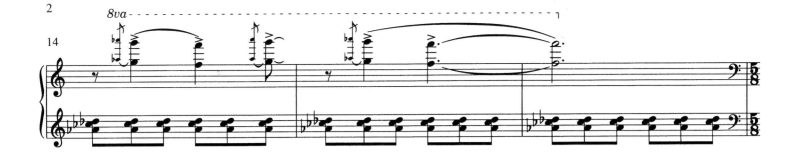

26 *with barely constrained excitement; almost breathless*

Those girls, _____ those girls,

28 those girls, ____ those ___ girls, ____

p grazioso

30 those girls, those love - ly sea - side girls. ____ Sharp as

33 nee - dles they are. Eyes ____ all o - ver them.

Long - ing to get the fright of their lives, _____ those

girls, those love - ly sea - side girls. _____

Al - low ___ me to in - tro - duce my.

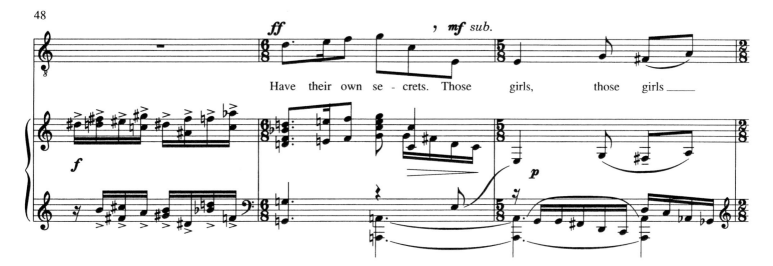

Have their own se - crets. Those girls, those girls ___

those girls, those girls, those sea - side ___ girls. ___

Chaps that would go to the

dogs____ if some__wo - man did - n't take them__ in hand.__

Wait. ____

Hm _____ Yes _____ that's her per -

fume. _____ What is it?____ He - li - o - trope? _____

8

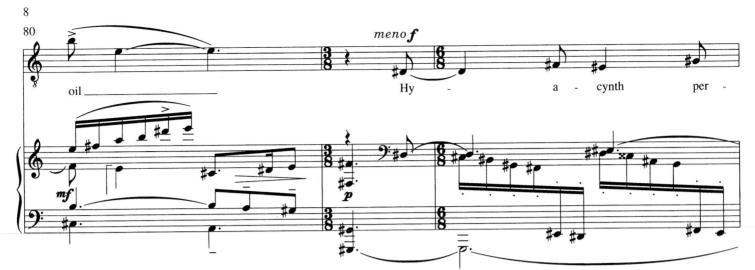

oil _____ Hy - a - cynth per -

fume made of oil ____ or e - ther or some - thing. ____

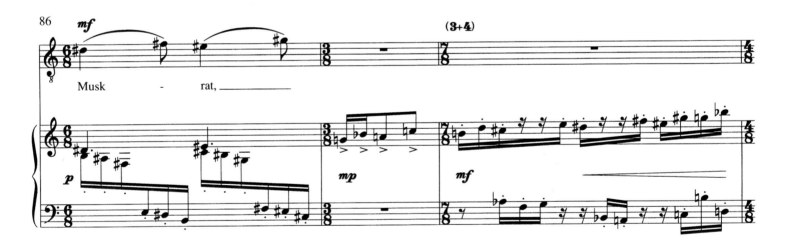

Musk - rat, ____

that's her per - fume. ___ Dogs at each

sniff?_____ Yes ____ now, look at it

that ____ way we're ____ the same. ____

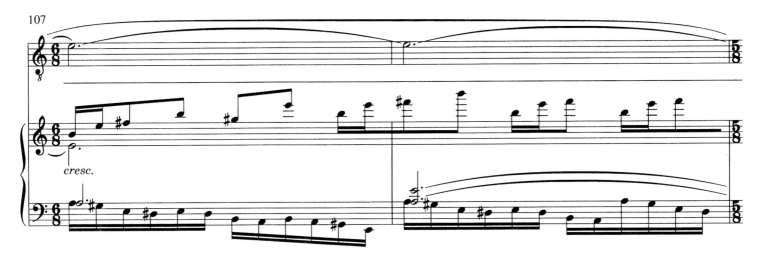

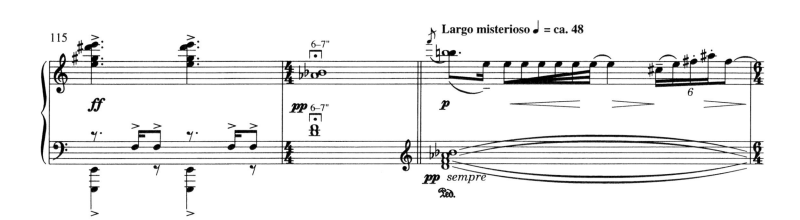

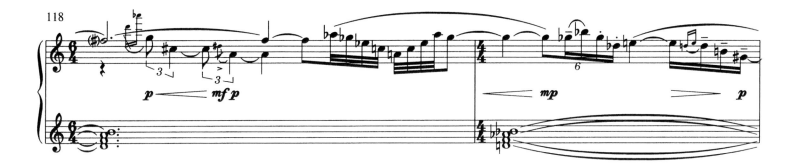

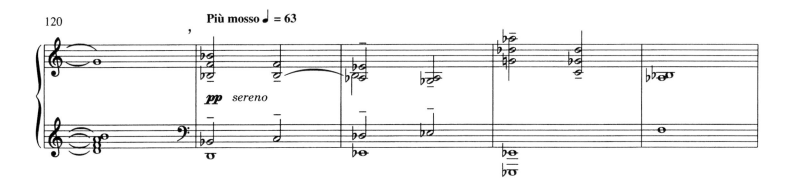

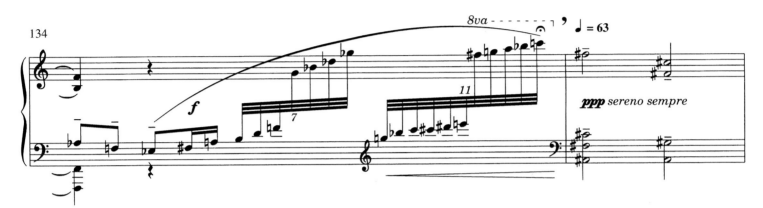

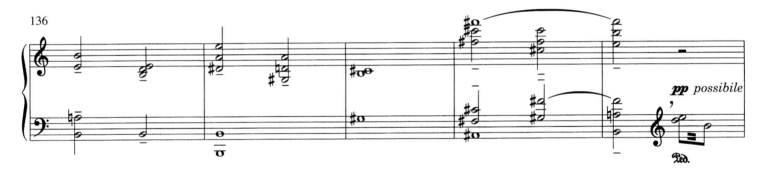

What is the mean-ing of _____ that _____ oth - er world? _____

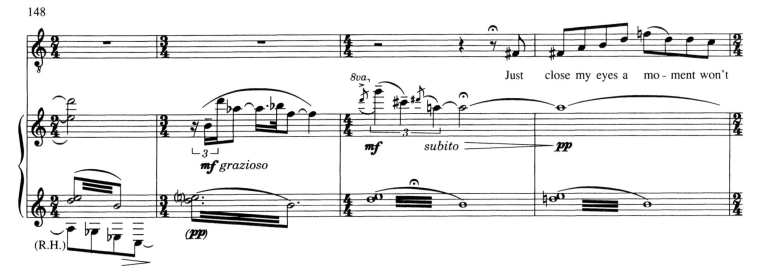

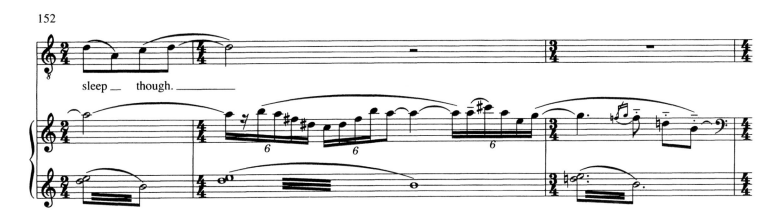

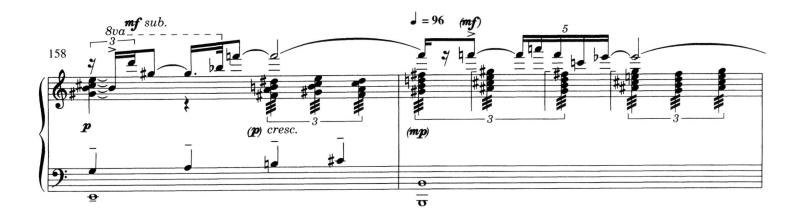

14

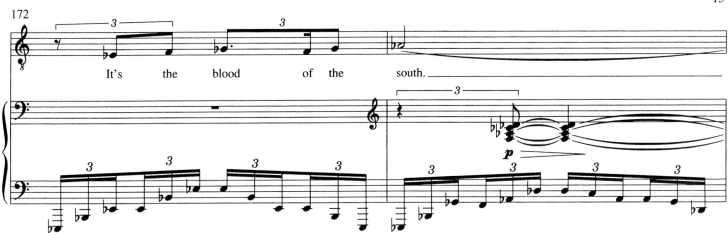

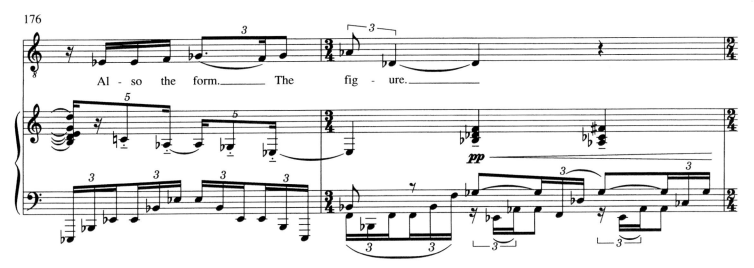

180

mf

kissed me. Kissed me.

182

Kissed me.

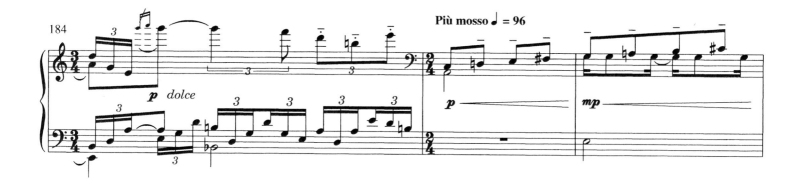

184

Più mosso ♩ = 96

p dolce

p

mp

187

ff martellato

mf

sim.

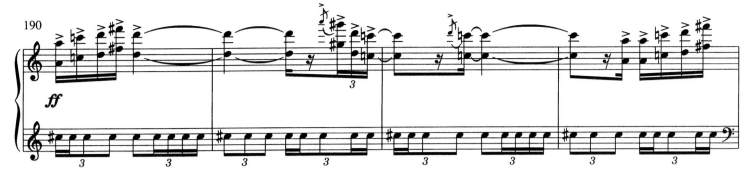

194 **Poco meno mosso**

Sun's ___ heat ___ it is ___ seems to a

se - cret touch ___ tell - ing me mem - o - ry. ___

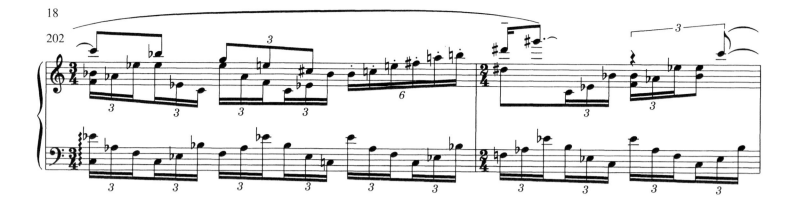

Below us bay __ sleep-ing sky. No sound. The sky. ____

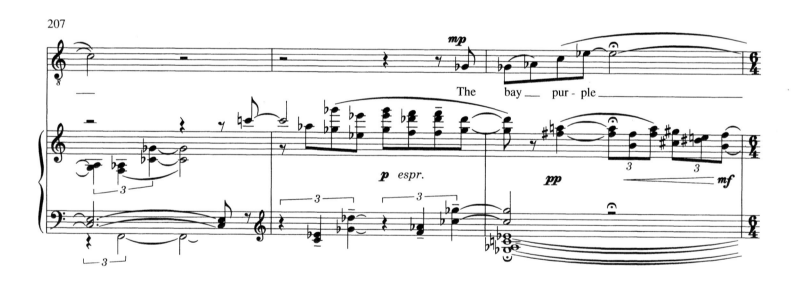

The bay __ pur-ple ____

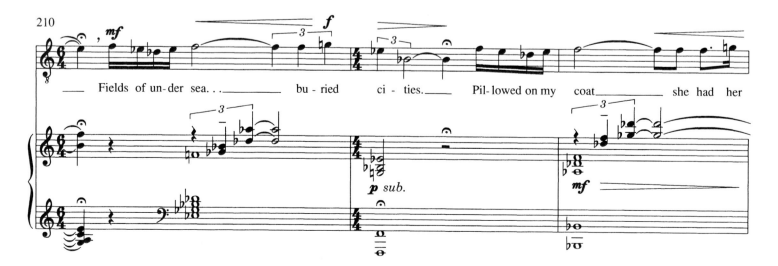

____ Fields of un-der sea... ____ bu-ried ci - ties. ____ Pil-lowed on my coat ____ she had her

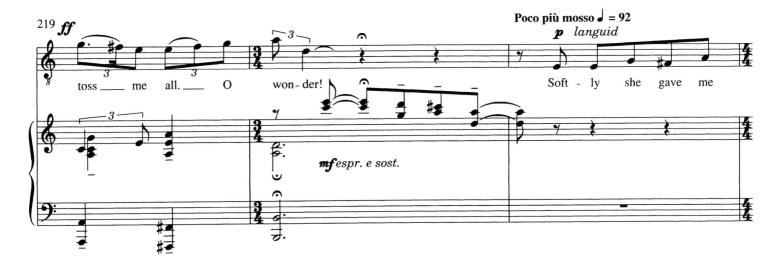

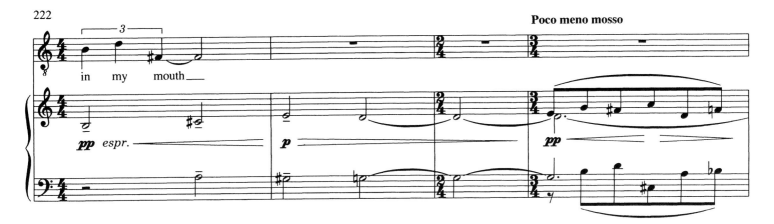

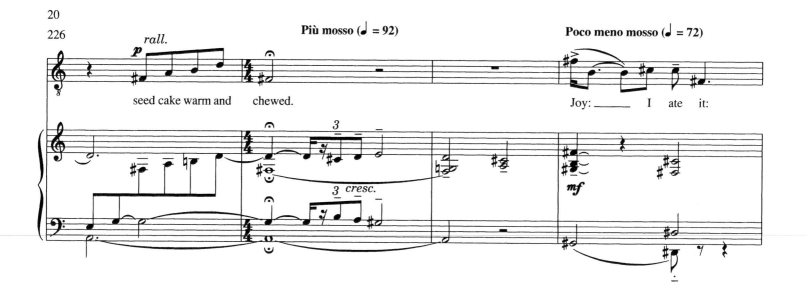

seed cake warm and chewed.

Joy: _____ I ate it:

Joy. _____

Young_ life _____ her lips that _____ gave _____ me pout-ing. _____

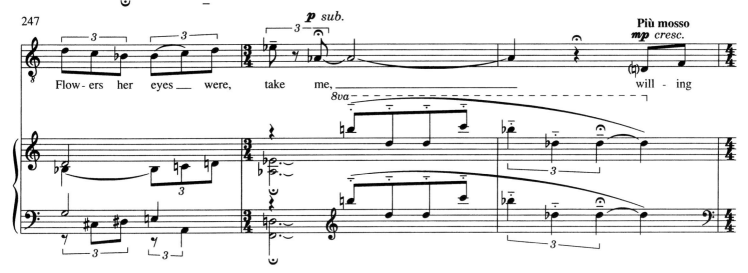

Flow-ers her eyes _____ were, take me, _____ will - ing

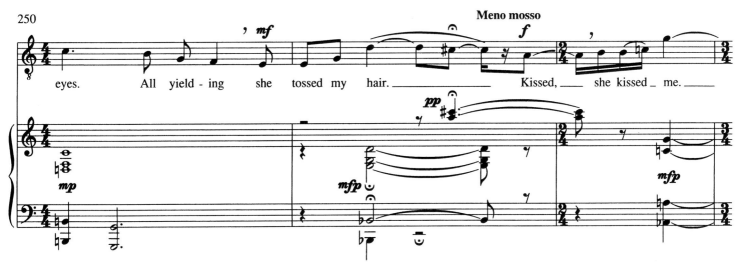

eyes. All yield-ing she tossed my hair. _____ Kissed, _____ she kissed _ me. _____

Will-ing eyes all yield - ing. _____

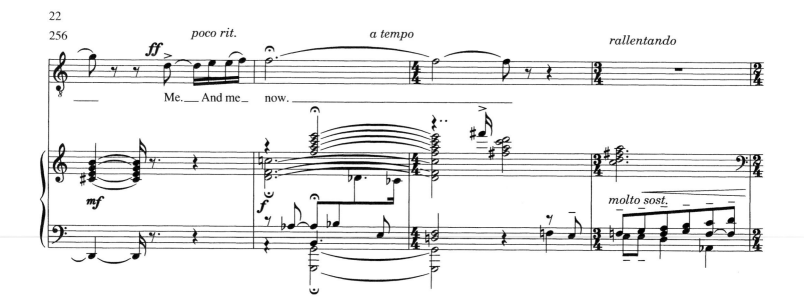

Me.___ And me___ now._____

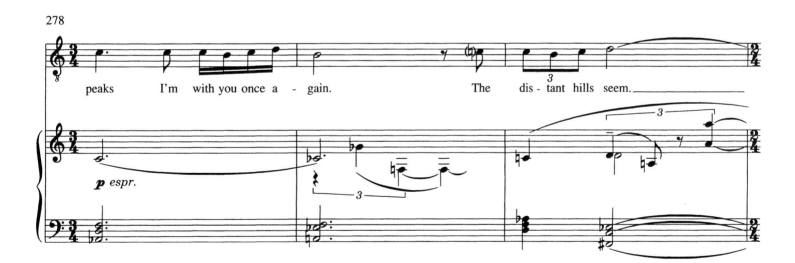
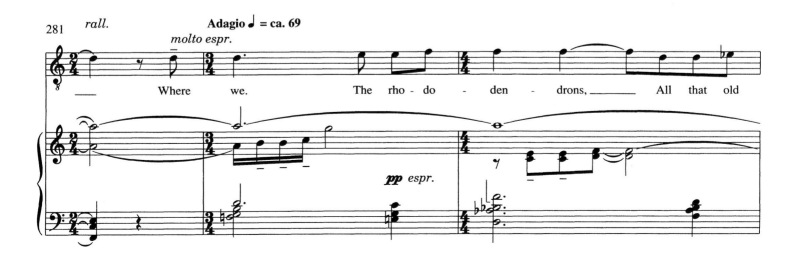

284

hill   has   seen.   All changed___ for-got-ten.___   And the dis-tant hills

288

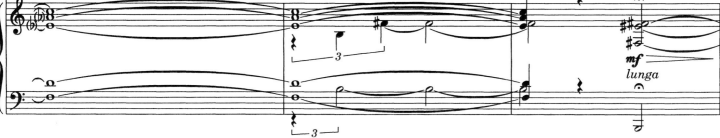

___   seem com - ing   nigh.___

291

with much feeling and wonder

A   star   I

292

see.___

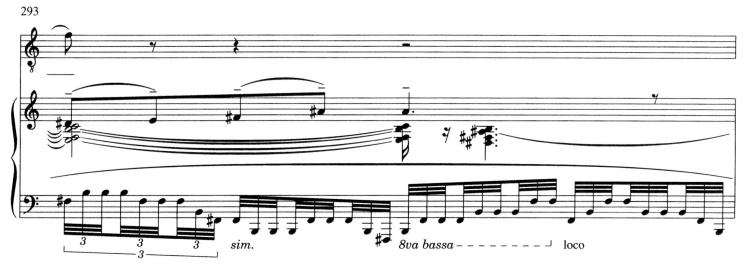

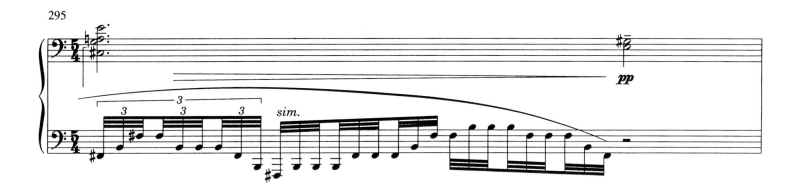

Were those night clouds those all the time?

No. Wait._____ Trees are

they?   Mi - rage._____

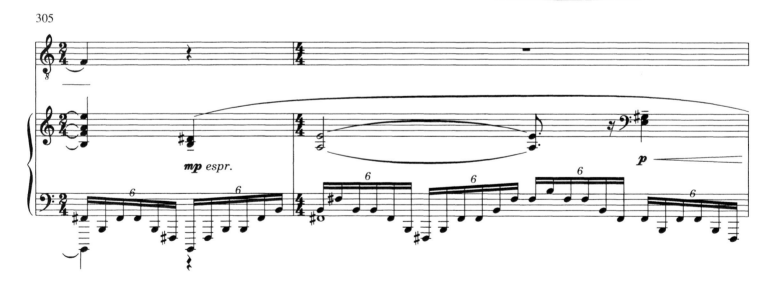

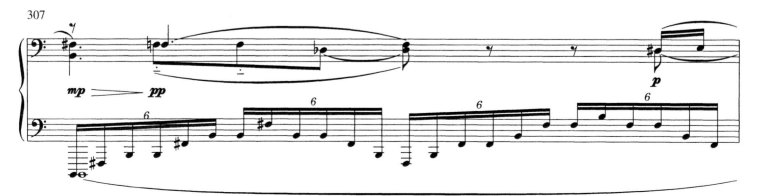